A Little Indulgence

TEA

Printed in the United States of America
by G&R Publishing Co.

Distributed By:

507 Industrial Street
Waverly, IA 50677

ISBN-13: 978-1-56383-217-8
ISBN-10: 1-56383-217-8
Item #6203

Drinking coffee is associated with the fast life we live, drinking wine conjures up thoughts of high society, and drinking spirits is often associated with those enjoying the wild nightlife. Drinking tea, however, is more of a Zen-like experience. Tea is peaceful, soothing, quiet and calming. In fact, in England, the entire world seems to stop for the afternoon tea. In Japan, drinking tea is an ageless tradition of beautiful ceremony. Throughout the world, almost every country enjoys some version of the steeped beverage, including America, which is the number one consumer of iced tea.

It is no surprise, then, that tea is the second most popular beverage in the world, second only to water. The story of tea goes back thousands of years. Tea united countries through open trading, fueled political fires through taxation and, at one time, was even used as currency in China.

Tea begins its life as leaves of the Camellia sinensis, an evergreen plant of the Camellia family. The smooth, shiny and pointed leaves of the evergreen are used to make all types of tea, including green, black and, the expensive and rare, white tea. Tea becomes an almost instant sensation to all who drink of its quenching flavor. Besides its quality to revive the thirsty and sustain energy among the weary, tea is often revered for its medicinal or health values. It is widely believed that drinking tea can help inhibit cardiovascular disease and certain forms of cancer. It can increase metabolism, helping to maintain good dental health and increased bone mass, as well as preventing premature aging. Whatever your reason for enjoying this multitalented beverage, brew up a fresh cup and turn the page to explore the world of tea…

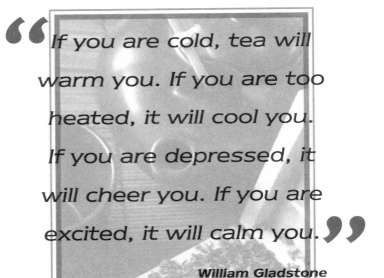

If you are cold, tea will warm you. If you are too heated, it will cool you. If you are depressed, it will cheer you. If you are excited, it will calm you.

William Gladstone

BOSTON ICED TEA
Makes 14 servings

1 gallon water
1 C. sugar
15 green or black tea bags

1 (12 oz.) can frozen
  cranberry juice
  concentrate

In a large pot over medium high heat, place water. Bring water to a boil and add sugar, stirring until sugar is completely dissolved. Add tea bags and steep until tea reaches desired strength. Remove from heat and stir in cranberry juice concentrate. Allow mixture to cool and serve in tall glasses over ice.

HERB LAVENDER TEA
Makes 4 servings

4 C. water
1 tsp. dried lavender
  flowers
1 tsp. dried chamomile
  flowers

1 tsp. green tea leaves
Honey, optional

In a medium saucepan over medium high heat, bring water to a boil. Meanwhile, fill a warmed teapot with dried lavender flowers, dried chamomile flowers and green tea leaves. Pour boiling water over tea mixture in pot. Cover and let steep for 3 to 5 minutes. To serve, pour tea through a tea strainer into cups. If desired, sweeten tea with honey.

CHAMOMILE TEA
Makes 2 servings

2 T. fresh chamomile
   flowers
2 thin slices apple

2 C. water
Honey, optional

Rinse flowers thoroughly under cool water and place in a warmed teapot. Slightly mash the apple slices and add to pot. In a small saucepan over medium high heat, bring water to a boil. Pour boiling water over mixture in pot. Cover and let steep for 3 to 5 minutes. To serve, pour tea through a tea strainer into cups. If desired, sweeten tea with honey.

THE FIRST CUP OF TEA

Tea has been around for thousands of years and, according to Chinese mythology, was first discovered by Chinese Emperor Shen Nung, a scholar and herbalist, around 2737 BC. According to the story, Shen Nung was sitting beneath a tree while his servants were boiling water to drink. Leaves from the tree dropped into the boiling water and Shen Nung decided to taste the dark brew. The tree was a wild tea tree. The Emperor found that the leaves left a delightful flavor to his water and this new discovery became his drink of favor.

An Indian legend tells of the story of Bodhidharma, a meditative Buddhist monk. According to the story, the monk suffered a seven-year period of sleepless contemplation. In desperation to fight off his tiredness, Bodhidharma chewed on some leaves from a nearby tea tree.

A Japanese myth speaks of the same Buddhist monk, Bodhidharma. The story tells how the monk, in his growing frustration at his inability to stay awake, threw his drooping eyelids to the ground. Tea bushes sprang up where his eyelids fell and the leaves of these new bushes miraculously cured his fatigue.

Though the Chinese myth holds the most weight for possible truth, China, India and Japan all claim the first invention of tea. There were, and still are, many reasons to want to claim this notorious discovery, including its religious value (tea was regarded as a drink to help the religious pray longer), for a plethora of medical virtues and because of its flavorful appeal. In fact, around 800 AD, tea was even used as currency in imperial China.

CLASSIC MINT ICED TEA
Makes 2 servings

2 C. water
4 tea bags
2 fresh mint sprigs or
½ tsp. dried mint leaves

Sugar to taste
2 lemon wedges for garnish

In a medium saucepan over medium heat, bring water to a boil. Remove from heat and add tea bags. Let tea steep to desired strength and mix in mint and sugar to taste, stirring until sugar is completely dissolved. Remove from heat and let cool, removing tea bags. To serve, fill two tall glasses with ice and pour tea mixture evenly into glasses. Garnish each glass with a lemon wedge.

BERRY SPICE ICED TEA
Makes 4 servings

3 C. water
3 cinnamon sticks
15 whole cloves
1½ C. cranberry juice

⅓ C. sugar
3 tsp. lemon juice
3 berry flavored tea bags

In a medium saucepan over medium high heat, bring water to a boil. Meanwhile, in a separate bowl, combine cinnamon sticks, whole cloves, cranberry juice, sugar and lemon juice. Pour boiling water over ingredients and add tea bags. Let tea steep to desired strength, removing tea bags as necessary. Cover bowl and set aside until cooled to room temperature. To serve, fill four tall glasses with ice and strain tea into glasses through a fine hole sieve to remove the cinnamon sticks and cloves.

SWEET GREEN TEA
Makes 2 servings

1 C. milk or soymilk
1 C. water
¼ C. brown sugar

½ tsp. cinnamon
¼ tsp. ground ginger
2 green tea bags

In a medium saucepan over medium heat, combine milk and water. Heat mixture just until it begins to gently boil. Stir in brown sugar, cinnamon, ground ginger and tea bags. Reduce heat and let simmer for about 3 minutes. Remove tea bags and pour mixture through a tea strainer into cups.

SPICED GINGER TEA

Makes 6 servings

6 C. water
4 ginger flavored tea bags
2 (3˝) pieces cinnamon
   stick

8 whole cloves
2 orange slices
4 tsp. honey or sugar

In a medium saucepan over medium high heat, bring water to a boil. Meanwhile, fill a warmed teapot with tea bags, cinnamon stick pieces, whole cloves and orange slices. Pour boiling water over tea mixture in pot. Cover and let steep for 3 minutes. Remove tea bags and stir in sweetener. Let steep for an additional 5 minutes. To serve, pour tea through a tea strainer into cups.

Strange how a teapot can represent at the same time the comforts of solitude and the pleasures of company.

Author Unknown

HOT OR COLD CHAI TEA
Makes 4 servings

2 C. water	5 whole cloves
4 black tea bags	¼ tsp. ground cardamom
¼ C. honey	¼ tsp. ground ginger
½ tsp. vanilla	Pinch of nutmeg
1 cinnamon stick	2 C. milk

In a medium saucepan over medium high heat, bring water to a boil. Add tea bags, honey and vanilla. Stir in cinnamon stick, whole cloves, ground cardamom, ground ginger and nutmeg. Reduce heat and let simmer for about 5 minutes. Add milk and return to a boil. To serve warm, remove tea bags and pour mixture through a tea strainer into cups. To serve cold, remove tea bags and strain into tall glasses filled with ice.

ALMOND LEMON TEA PUNCH
Makes 12 servings

2 (7 oz.) large tea bags
4 C. water
2 lemons, thinly sliced
1 C. sugar

1 T. almond extract
2 tsp. vanilla
1 (2 liter) bottle lemon
  lime soda, chilled

In a medium saucepan over medium heat, bring water to a boil. Reduce heat to a low simmer and add tea bags. Let tea bags steep for about 15 minutes. Place sliced lemons and sugar in a large pitcher, squeezing lemon slices as they are added. Remove tea bags and pour tea mixture into pitcher. Stir until sugar is completely dissolved and place in refrigerator for 1 day. Before serving, mix in almond extract, vanilla and lemon lime soda. To serve, pour tea punch over ice in glasses.

SIMPLE SOUTHERN TEA
Makes 1 gallon

3 (7 oz.) large tea bags   **2 C. sugar**

In a coffee maker, place tea bags in the strainer basket where you would normally place the coffee filter. Add water to coffee maker and brew as normal. Place sugar in a large pitcher and fill with hot brewed tea. Continue to brew tea until there is enough tea to fill the pitcher. Mix with a long spoon until sugar is completely dissolved. Let tea cool completely to room temperature and place in refrigerator until ready to serve. To serve, pour tea over ice in tall glasses.

HONEY LEMON TEA

Makes 1 serving

1 C. water
2 tsp. honey

1 tsp. fresh lemon juice
1 tea bag

Place water in a microwave-safe mug. Stir in honey and heat in microwave for 1½ minutes. Remove from microwave and stir in lemon juice, mixing until honey is completely dissolved. Add tea bag and let steep for 2 to 3 minutes. Let cool slightly before serving.

ANISE TEA
Makes 1 serving

1 C. water   **1 tsp. honey**
1 tsp. dried anise leaves

In a small saucepan over medium high heat, bring water to a boil. Meanwhile, fill a warmed teapot with dried anise leaves. Pour boiling water over leaves in pot. Cover and let steep for 3 to 5 minutes. To serve, pour tea through a tea strainer into a cup. Add honey and stir until honey is completely dissolved.

GREEN BUBBLE TEA
Makes 1 serving

2 C. water
5 tsp. sugar, divided
⅓ C. pearl tapioca

1 C. brewed green tea, cold
2 T. milk
1 C. ice cubes

In a small saucepan over medium heat, bring water to a boil. Stir in 1 teaspoon sugar, mixing well until sugar is completely dissolved. Reduce heat and add pearl tapioca. Continue heating for about 30 to 40 minutes, watching carefully. Remove from heat, rinse tapioca under cool water and drain. Place tapioca in refrigerator to chill. In a cocktail shaker, combine cold tea, milk and remaining 4 teaspoons sugar. Shake vigorously and add ice cubes. Strain mixture into a glass and stir in tapioca. Mix lightly. Serve with a large straw to draw up the tapioca as you drink.

ICED STRAWBERRY TEA
Makes 4 servings

1 pint fresh strawberries   ⅓ **C. sugar**
4 C. brewed tea, cold   ¼ **C. fresh lemon juice**

Set aside four whole strawberries. Wash and hull the remaining strawberries. In a blender or food processor, place hulled strawberries. Process on high until strawberries are pureed. Pour strawberry puree into a pitcher through a strainer. Stir in cold tea, sugar and lemon juice. Mix until sugar is completely dissolved. Chill in refrigerator until ready to serve. To serve, fill four tall glasses with ice. Pour tea mixture over ice and garnish each glass with one of the reserved whole strawberries.

TEA TIMELINE

400 – 600 AD
The demand for tea rose steadily. Farmers began to cultivate tea, rather than harvest leaves from wild trees.

805
Buddhist monk, Saicho, brought tea seeds from Japan to China.

1206 – 1368
Genghis Khan and Kublai Khan conquered Chinese territories and established a Mongolian dynasty. Tea fell from high status and became an ordinary drink.

1610
The Dutch traded dried sage for tea in China and brought the drink to Europe.

2737 BC | 400 – 600 AD | 780 | 805 | 960 – 1280 | 1206 – 1368 | 1368 – 1644 | 1422 – 1502 | 1610

2737 BC
Shen Nung, the Second Emperor of China, discovered tea.

960 – 1280
Powdered tea became common and beautiful ceramic tea accessories became popular.

1422 – 1502
The Zen priest, Murata Shuko, created the Japanese tea ceremony, which is called "Cha No Yu", meaning "hot water for tea".

780
Chinese author, Lu Yu, wrote the first book on tea "Ch'a Ching". It comprises three inclusive volumes, covering everything from the growth of tea to its historical summary, as well as utensils for making tea.

1368 – 1644
The Ming dynasty in China. People began to, once again, enjoy tea. The new method of preparation was steeping whole tea leaves in water. Lighter colored ceramic was developed in order to see the resulting pale liquid.

1833
The East India Company enjoyed its monopoly on the tea trade for 250 years. Independent merchants campaigned for change and modernization, which was achieved in 1833.

1918
A National Tea Control was brought in and tea was split into three grades and sold at a fixed retail price.

1657
Tea was first sold in England at Garway's Coffee House in London.

1870
Tea companies blossomed in Britain and gave customers a wide variety of choices by blending, branding and packaging tea themselves.

1657   1705   1773   1833   1870   1904   1909   1918   1940   2003

1773
The Tea Act of 1773 gave the East India Company control of trading in the Americas, imposing taxes and levies on the colonists. Objection to the Act led to the infamous Boston Tea Party.

1909
Thomas Sullivan invented tea bags by mistake. He sent tea to clients in New York wrapped in silk bags, which they steeped in hot water without opening.

2003
India is the country with the most tea consumption in the world, averaging 651,000 metric tons per year. The USA is the number one consumer of iced tea, consuming between 80% and 85% of our total tea in that manner.

1705
The yearly importation of tea grew to approximately 800,000 pounds in England.

1904
Richard Blechynden created iced tea for the St. Louis World Fair.

1940
After a slump in the tea trade, Britain and the UK began to recover. However, the economy collapsed with World War II and tea was rationed from 1940 until October 1952.

FRIENDSHIP TEA
Makes 40 servings

½ C. instant tea powder
1 C. sweetened lemonade powder

1 C. Tang
1 tsp. cinnamon
½ tsp. ground cloves

In a large bowl, combine instant tea powder, sweetened lemonade powder, Tang, cinnamon and ground cloves. Mix well until fully incorporated. Transfer mixture to an airtight container. To prepare one serving, place 2 to 3 teaspoons tea mixture in a mug. Pour 1 cup boiling water over mixture in mug and stir until completely dissolved. Add more or less tea mixture to taste. Let cool slightly before serving.

COLD CRANBERRY TEA
Makes 12 servings

3 tsp. instant tea powder
½ tsp. allspice
½ tsp. cinnamon
½ tsp. nutmeg
6 C. boiling water

1 (3 oz.) pkg. cherry gelatin
1 C. orange juice
¼ C. lemon juice
1 qt. cranberry juice
½ C. sugar

Fill a piece of cheesecloth with instant tea powder, all-spice, cinnamon and nutmeg. Close cheesecloth bag with a piece of kitchen twine. In a large saucepan over medium high heat, bring water to a boil. Add cheesecloth filled with spices and let steep for 5 minutes. Stir in cherry gelatin, remove from heat and let cool to room temperature. Mix in orange juice, lemon juice, cranberry juice and sugar, mixing well until sugar is completely dissolved. To serve, pour tea into tall glasses filled with ice.

CHAI TEA MIX
Makes 36 servings

1 C. dry milk powder
1 C. powdered non-dairy creamer
1 C. French vanilla flavored powder creamer
2½ C. sugar

1½ C. instant tea powder
2 tsp. ground ginger
2 tsp. cinnamon
1 tsp. ground cloves
1 tsp. ground cardamom

In a large bowl, combine dry milk powder, non-dairy creamer, French vanilla powdered creamer, sugar and instant tea powder. Mix until well incorporated. Add ground ginger, cinnamon, ground cloves and ground cardamom. Stir until fully mixed. Place 1 cup of the tea mixture in a blender or food processor. Process until tea mix is a fine powder. Repeat with remaining mixture, blending 1 cup at a time. To prepare one serving, place 2 tablespoons tea mixture in a mug. Pour 1 cup boiling water over mixture in mug and stir until completely dissolved. Let cool slightly before serving.

"*Drink your tea slowly and reverently, as if it is the axis on which the world earth revolves – slowly, evenly, without rushing toward the future.*"

Thich Nat Hahn

PASSION PINEAPPLE FROSTY
Makes 10 servings

4 passion fruit flavored
  tea bags
1 C. cold water
3 C. ice cubes

⅓ C. sugar
2 C. fresh chopped
  pineapple
1 large banana, sliced

In a medium saucepan over medium high heat, bring water to a boil. Add tea bags and let steep for 5 minutes. Remove from heat and discard tea bags, draining any liquid from tea bags back into saucepan. In a blender, combine brewed tea, sugar, chopped pineapple and banana slices. Pulse until slightly blended and add ice cubes. Puree until mixture is a frosty slush. Pour into glasses and serve immediately.

APPLE JUICE PUNCH
Makes 6 to 8 servings

3 C. water
4 black tea bags
⅓ C. honey

3 C. unsweetened
  apple juice
Lemon slices for garnish

In a large saucepan over medium high heat, bring water to a boil. Add tea bags and let steep for 3 to 5 minutes. Remove from heat and discard tea bags. Let tea cool to room temperature and mix in honey and apple juice. Stir well and pour into tall glasses filled with ice. Garnish each serving with a lemon slice.

BLUEBERRY TEATIME SMOOTHIE

Makes 2 servings

1 Irish Breakfast tea bag
1 C. boiling water
1 C. frozen blueberries
½ C. apple juice

¼ C. plain yogurt
1 T. honey
1 C. ice cubes

In a small teapot, place Irish Breakfast tea bag and boiling water. Let tea steep in water for about 10 minutes and chill in refrigerator until cool. Set aside a few whole blueberries for garnish. Meanwhile, in a blender, combine remaining blueberries, apple juice, plain yogurt, cold tea and honey. Process on high speed until well blended and smooth. Add ice and blend until well combined. To serve, pour mixture evenly into a two tall glasses and garnish with reserved whole blueberries.

STRAWBERRY YOGURT COOLER

Makes 2 servings

2 rosehip tea bags
2 C. boiling water
2 C. plain yogurt

3 T. honey
1 C. sliced strawberries

In a small teapot, place rosehip tea bags and boiling water. Let tea steep in water for about 10 minutes. Meanwhile, in a blender, combine brewed tea, plain yogurt, honey and sliced strawberries. Process on high speed until well blended and smooth. To serve, pour mixture evenly into a two tall glasses filled with ice.

FRUI-TEA PUNCH
Makes 6 servings

1 C. honey
1 C. orange juice
½ C. fresh lemon juice
½ C. crushed
   strawberries
½ C. crushed blueberries

1½ C. strong brewed tea
1 pint ginger ale
Crushed ice
Whole blueberries for
   garnish

In a tall pitcher, combine honey, orange juice, lemon juice, crushed strawberries, crushed blueberries and strong brewed tea. Mix until well combined and add ginger ale and crushed ice. If punch is too strong, dilute mixture by adding water. To serve, pour into glasses and garnish each glass with a few whole blueberries.

GINSENG TOMATO JUICE COCKTAIL
Makes 6 servings

2 C. cold water
5 green tea with ginseng
   bags
4 C. tomato juice
½ tsp. ground ginger

½ tsp. celery salt,
   optional
1 tsp. Tabasco sauce,
   optional
Celery stalks

In a medium saucepan over medium high heat, bring water to a rapid boil. Add tea bags and let steep for 7 minutes. Remove from heat and discard tea bags. Let tea cool to room temperature. In a large pitcher, place tomato juice, ground ginger and, if desired, celery salt and Tabasco sauce. Add brewed tea and mix until well incorporated. Chill in refrigerator for 2 hours. To serve, pour tomato juice cocktail into tall glasses and garnish each glass with a celery stalk.

THE BOSTON TEA PARTY

In 1773, Britain's East India Company faced bankruptcy, as they sat on a large stock of tea that would not sell in England. In an effort to save the company, the government passed the Tea Act of 1773, allowing the company to export its merchandise directly to the new colonies in America without paying any of the regular taxes that were imposed on colonial merchants. With this new law, the East India Company would be allowed to monopolize the colonial tea trade, underselling American merchants. Further resentment was created when the East India Company granted franchises to only a few American merchants for the sale of their tea.

The Prime Minister of Britain assumed the colonists would welcome the new law because it would reduce the price of tea to the consumers. The colonists linked

together to boycott tea, joining much
of the population together in a common experience of
mass protest.

Some of the colonies made plans to prevent the
East India Company from landing ships in colonial ports.
New shipments of tea were either returned or warehoused.
Many agents of the company were persuaded to resign.
The agents in Boston refused to resign but, with the
support of the Massachusetts governor, preparations
were made for incoming cargo ships to land, regardless
of the opposition.

After three ships landing in Boston refused to
turn back, local patriots, led by Samuel Adams,
staged a rebellion. On the evening of December 16, 1773, three groups of 50 men dressed
as Mohawk Indians boarded the ships, broke
open tea chests and threw 45 tons of
tea into the harbor. As the news spread,
other ports up and down the coast
staged similar acts of resistance.

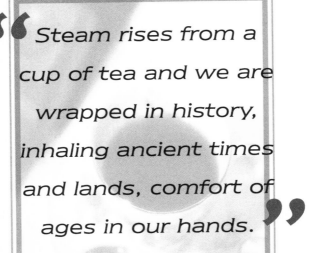

Steam rises from a cup of tea and we are wrapped in history, inhaling ancient times and lands, comfort of ages in our hands.

Faith Greenbowl

FROZEN SUMMER SLUSH
Makes 20 servings

2 C. sugar
9 C. cold water, divided
2 T. instant tea powder
1 (12 oz.) can frozen
   orange juice concentrate

1 (12 oz.) can frozen
   lemonade concentrate
2 C. vodka
1 liter lemon lime soda

In a large pot over medium high heat, combine sugar and 7 cups water. Bring to a boil, stirring occasionally, until sugar is completely dissolved. Remove from heat and mix in instant tea powder. Stir until tea is completely dissolved and add frozen orange juice concentrate, frozen lemonade concentrate and remaining 2 cups cold water. Mix well and place in refrigerator to chill. When liquid is cold, mix in vodka. Pour mixture into a large freezer container and place in freezer for 24 hours. For each serving, scoop about 1 cup frozen mixture into a tall glass and add 1/3 cup lemon lime soda. Mix lightly and serve.

APRICOT BRANDY SLUSH

Makes 35 servings

8 C. water
2 C. sugar
4 black or green tea bags
2 (12 oz.) cans frozen
   orange juice
   concentrate, thawed

2 (12 oz.) cans frozen
   lemonade concentrate,
   thawed
13 oz. apricot brandy

In a large saucepan over medium high heat, bring water to a boil. Add sugar and stir until sugar is completely dissolved. Remove from heat and add tea bags. Let tea steep for 8 hours or overnight at room temperature. In a large freezer container, combine tea mixture, orange juice concentrate, lemonade concentrate and apricot brandy. Cover tightly and place in freezer, stirring every 2 hours, until completely frozen. To serve, let mixture thaw at room temperature for 5 to 10 minutes. Break up slush with a fork and scoop into glasses to serve.

BLACK TEA STRAWBERRY PUNCH
Makes 34 servings

1 (10 oz.) pkg. frozen
  sliced strawberries in
  syrup
1 (12 oz.) can frozen
  orange juice
  concentrate, thawed
1 (12 oz.) can frozen
  lemonade concentrate,
  thawed

8 C. water
2 C. brewed black tea
2 C. sugar
3 C. light rum
24 ice cubes
2 (2 liter) bottles lemon
  lime soda, chilled

In a large punch bowl, combine strawberries in syrup, orange juice concentrate, lemonade concentrate, water and tea. Mix until strawberries are broken up and ingredients are well combined. Mix in sugar and rum. Add ice cubes and mix in lemon lime soda. Stir lightly and serve immediately.

PINEAPPLE BOURBON SLUSH

Makes 14 servings

1 (6 oz.) can frozen orange juice concentrate, thawed

1 (12 oz.) can frozen lemonade concentrate, thawed

1 (46 oz.) can pineapple juice

1½ C. sugar

2 C. strong brewed black tea

2 C. bourbon whiskey

1 (2 liter) bottle lemon lime soda

14 maraschino cherries

In a large bowl, mix together orange juice concentrate, lemonade concentrate, pineapple juice, sugar, tea and bourbon whiskey. Mix well and transfer mixture to shallow bowls, cover and place in freezer for 8 hours or overnight. Remove mixture from freezer and let stand for 10 minutes. Using a wire whisk or potato masher, mash frozen mixture to make a slushy consistency. Scoop slush into glasses and pour lemon lime soda over each serving. Garnish each serving with a maraschino cherry.

SANGRIA TEA
Makes 9 servings

1 (10 oz.) pkg. frozen
   raspberries, thawed
3 C. water
1/3 C. sugar
1 (7 oz.) large tea bag

2 C. red grape juice
1 lemon, sliced
1 lime, sliced
1 (16 oz.) bottle orange
   soda, chilled

In a blender or food processor, process raspberries at high speed until smooth. Pour raspberry puree through a fine hole sieve into a large pitcher, discarding raspberry seeds. Set raspberry puree aside. In a large saucepan over medium high heat, bring water and sugar to a boil, stirring often. Remove from heat and add tea bag. Cover and let tea steep for 5 minutes. Remove tea bag, draining any liquid from tea bag back into saucepan. Let tea mixture cool to room temperature. Once cooled, add tea mixture to raspberry puree in pitcher. Mix in grape juice, lemon slices and lime slices. Mix well and chill in refrigerator. Before serving, mix in orange soda and serve in tall glasses over ice.

"Tea's proper use is to amuse the idle, and relax the studious, and dilute the full meals of those who cannot use exercise, and will not use abstinence."

Samuel Johnson

HOT HOLIDAY CIDER
Makes 6 servings

1 qt. water
3 orange spice tea bags
½ C. brown sugar
2 C. apple cider

1½ C. light rum
8 cinnamon sticks, divided
3 tsp. butter, divided

In a large saucepan over medium high heat, bring water to a boil. Remove from heat and add orange spice tea bags. Cover and let steep for 5 minutes. Remove tea bags and stir in brown sugar, apple cider, light rum and 2 cinnamon sticks. Return mixture to heat and bring to just steaming, being careful not to boil. To serve, ladle cider into 6 mugs and drop ½ teaspoon butter into each. Garnish each serving with 1 remaining cinnamon stick.

MINT TEA PUNCH
Makes 10 servings

3 C. boiling water
12 sprigs fresh mint
4 black or green tea bags
1 C. sugar
1 C. orange juice

¼ C. lemon juice
5 C. cold water
3 orange slices, optional
3 lemon slices, optional

In a large pitcher, place fresh mint sprigs and tea bags. Pour boiling water over mint and tea bags and let steep for 8 minutes. Remove tea bags, draining any liquid from tea bags back into pitcher. Mix in sugar, stirring until sugar is completely dissolved. Add orange juice, lemon juice and cold water. Mix well and pour into tall glasses over ice. If desired, garnish with orange and lemon slices.

APPLE CINNAMON SHAKES
Makes 2 servings

4 C. vanilla ice cream
½ tsp. cinnamon

3 apple cinnamon tea bags
Whipped topping, optional

In a blender, place vanilla ice cream and cinnamon. Carefully cut open tea bags and add loose tea from bags to the blender. Process on high until well incorporated. To serve, pour shakes evenly into two tall glasses. If desired, top with a dollop of whipped topping.

FRUIT GREEN TEA SMOOTHIE

Makes 2 to 4 servings

1 peach, sliced
1 apple, sliced
1 C. frozen red grapes
1 C. frozen blueberries

1½ C. frozen sliced
strawberries
1 C. hot brewed green tea

In a blender, combine peach slices, apple slices, frozen grapes, frozen blueberries and frozen sliced strawberries. Pour hot brewed tea over fruit in blender. Process until smooth and pour into glasses to serve.

HOT GROG
Makes 1 serving

1 oz. cognac
1 oz. dark rum
1 C. brewed tea
5 whole cloves

½ tsp. honey
Pinch of nutmeg
1 cinnamon stick

In a medium saucepan over medium heat, combine cognac, dark rum, brewed tea, whole cloves, honey and nutmeg. Heat for 1 to 2 minutes, stirring frequently, until mixture is well blended and begins to steam. Pour mixture into a mug and garnish with a cinnamon stick.

TYPES OF TEA

There are five categories of tea: black, oolong, green, white and pu'erh. All five types come from the Camellia sinensis plant and the category is determined by the type of process the leaves undergo once harvested.

BLACK TEA

After picking, leaves undergo five stages of very precise processing in order to produce black tea. The leaves are spread on a mesh screen to dry and then rolled by hand or machines to release essential oils. The leaves are then placed on mats and sorted by size and type to determine the grade. The leaves undergo fermentation, or oxidation, which includes heating and then cooling. Finally, the leaves are dried or fired in a large pan. Black tea generally produces a dark red or brown liquid and has a smooth, yet strong taste. Black tea contains the most amount of caffeine, though a typical cup contains about half the caffeine of coffee.

OOLONG TEA

In terms of processing and taste, oolong tea falls between black and green tea, and therefore, shares the qualities of both black and green tea. The drying and fermentation stages of processing are combined. Oolong tea creates a semifermented brew containing less caffeine than black tea.

GREEN TEA

Green tea is made from unfermented leaves. More of the leaves' beneficial properties remain intact because they undergo less processing. Some green teas are light and mild tasting, while others can have a bitter or grassy taste.

WHITE TEA

Made from the fresh buds of the Camellia plant, white tea is the purest of all teas. It is very rare and enjoyed mostly by tea connoisseurs. A premium white tea can cost $120 or more per pound.

PU'ERH TEA

A favorite of China, pu'erh tea is believed to contain many medicinal qualities, including aiding digestion and reducing cholesterol. Pu'erh is the only tea that is aged before processing. Premium pu'erh teas are sometimes aged for 20 to 60 years.

TEA EGG NOG

Makes 8 servings

6 black or green tea bags
2 eggs, beaten
1 (14 oz.) can sweetened
   condensed milk
1 tsp. vanilla

¼ tsp. salt
4 C. milk
1 C. whipped topping
Nutmeg for garnish

In a large glass measuring cup, place 1 cup water. Heat in microwave for 1 minute. Add tea bags and let tea steep for 5 minutes. Remove tea bags, squeezing any excess liquid from bags back into measuring cup. Let tea cool to room temperature. In a blender, combine cold tea, beaten eggs, sweetened condensed milk, vanilla, salt and milk. Process on high for a few seconds, until well blended. Pour mixture evenly into 8 glasses and top with whipped topping. Sprinkle a pinch of nutmeg over each serving for garnish.

Warning: Eating raw eggs is not recommended for pregnant women, the elderly and the sick because there is a risk that eggs may be contaminated with salmonella bacteria.

WASSAIL TEA PUNCH
Makes 12 servings

4 C. hot brewed tea
1 C. sugar
1 (32 oz.) bottle cranberry juice
1 (32 oz.) bottle apple juice

2 C. orange juice
¾ C. lemon juice
2 cinnamon sticks
24 whole cloves, divided
1 orange, sliced

In a large pot over medium high heat, combine brewed tea and sugar. Mix well and add cranberry juice, apple juice, orange juice, lemon juice, cinnamon sticks and 12 whole cloves. Bring mixture to a boil for 2 minutes, stirring occasionally. Remove from heat and transfer mixture to a large punch bowl. Press remaining 12 whole cloves into orange slices and add to punch bowl. Punch can be served hot or cold.

ALMOND-TEA SHAKES

Makes 8 servings

⅓ C. sugar
⅔ C. water
4 C. milk
¾ C. corn syrup

1½ C. blanched slivered
   almonds, toasted*
1 C. brewed black tea, cold

In a small saucepan over medium high heat, combine sugar and water. Bring mixture to a boil, stirring constantly, until sugar is completely dissolved. Add milk, corn syrup and toasted almonds, stirring well. Remove from heat and chill mixture in refrigerator for 8 hours or overnight. In a blender, place almond mixture. Process until mixture is smooth and pour mixture into a freezer container through a fine hole sieve. Remove almond bits and place strained liquid in freezer for 3 hours, stirring occasionally. To serve, place half of the frozen mixture in a blender and add half of the brewed tea. Process until well blended and smooth. Pour into glasses and repeat with remaining frozen mixture and tea.

* To toast, place slivered almonds in a single layer
on a baking sheet. Bake at 350° for approximately 10 minutes
or until almonds are golden brown.

CHOCOLATE CHAI
Makes 8 to 10 servings

4 Darjeeling, English
   breakfast or Lapsang
   Souchong tea bags
2 C. boiling water
¾ C. sugar
½ C. cocoa powder
8 C. milk

1 T. vanilla
2 tsp. cinnamon
2 tsp. nutmeg
Whipped topping
Candy canes for garnish,
   optional

In a large saucepan over medium heat, place tea bags. Add boiling water, cover and let steep for 3 to 5 minutes. Remove tea bags, squeezing any excess liquid back into saucepan, and stir in sugar and cocoa powder. Continue to heat until mixture begins to boil. Reduce heat slightly and stir in milk, vanilla, cinnamon and nutmeg, stirring until mixture is heated throughout, being careful not to boil. Divide hot tea into mugs and serve each with a dollop of whipped topping. If desired, garnish each serving with a candy cane.

ORANGE TEA JELLY

Makes 6 pints

1¾ C. water
12 Orange Pekoe tea bags
¼ C. orange juice

3 C. sugar
1 (3 oz.) pkg. liquid pectin

In a large saucepan over medium high heat, bring water to a boil. Add Orange Pekoe tea bags and let tea steep for 30 minutes. Remove from heat and discard tea bags. Add orange juice and sugar to tea mixture and return to heat. Bring to a boil for 2 minutes, stirring constantly. Remove from heat and stir in liquid pectin. Return to heat and bring to a boil for 1 minute. Skim foam off top of mixture and ladle hot jelly into pint jars that have been heated and sterilized. Pour jelly mixture to within ½" of the top of each jar. Close each jar tightly with a 2-piece lid. Place filled, closed jars in a pan of boiling water for 15 minutes.

GARLIC LEMON SEASONING RUB

Makes 2 to 3 tablespoons

3 lemon flavored green
    tea bags
1 tsp. garlic powder

1 tsp. pepper
¼ tsp. grated lemon peel

Cut open tea bags and pour contents of tea bags into a ziplock bag. Add garlic powder, pepper and grated lemon peel. Seal bag and mix contents by shaking vigorously. Use seasoning as a rub for whitefish, bluefish, pork chops or shrimp before grilling or broiling. Store leftover seasoning rub in a dark, cool place.

RASPBERRY VINAIGRETTE DRESSING
Makes 3 cups

20 raspberry flavored
   tea bags
2 C. balsamic vinegar
½ C. extra virgin olive oil
½ C. water

1 tsp. dried rosemary
1 tsp. dried thyme
½ tsp. pepper
1½ tsp. minced garlic

In a 1-quart glass jar, place tea bags. Pour vinegar, olive oil and water over tea bags. Close jar securely and shake vigorously. Place in refrigerator and chill for 24 hours, shaking occasionally. Remove tea bags, draining any liquid from tea bags back into glass jar. Add dried rosemary, dried thyme, pepper and minced garlic to jar, close and shake well. Use vinaigrette over salad greens, tossed with hot or cold pasta or as a marinade for chicken, shrimp or pork. Refrigerate after use and discard after 10 days.

"There are those who love
to get dirty and fix things.
They drink coffee at dawn,
beer after work. And
those who stay clean,
just appreciate things. At
breakfast they have milk and
juice at night. There are those
who do both, they drink tea."

Gary Snyder

GREEN TEA CHERRY DESSERT SAUCE

Makes 1 cup

1 C. cold water
10 green cherry flavored
   tea bags

4 T. butter
2 T. sugar
2 T. brown sugar

In a small saucepan over medium high heat, bring water to a boil. Add tea bags and let steep for 7 minutes. Remove from heat and discard tea bags, draining any liquid from tea bags back into saucepan. In a separate saucepan over low heat, place butter. Heat until butter is melted and stir in tea, sugar and brown sugar. Increase heat and bring to a boil, stirring constantly. Reduce heat and let simmer for 2 minutes. Use as a sauce to drizzle over ice cream, fresh fruit or angel food cake. Refrigerate after use.

TEA LEAF SHORTBREAD

Makes about 5 dozen

1½ C. butter
1 tsp. vanilla
1¼ C. sugar, divided
2 T. loose tea leaves

3 C. flour
¾ tsp. salt
1 large egg
1 T. cold water

In a medium bowl, cream together butter, vanilla and 1 cup sugar. When mixture is smooth, mix in loose tea leaves, flour and salt, mixing until well combined. Roll out dough into two 12″ logs, about 1½″ in diameter. Wrap logs in plastic wrap and chill in refrigerator for 1 hour. Preheat oven to 350°. Lightly grease a baking sheet. In a small bowl, combine egg and cold water, mixing well. Unwrap logs and, using a pastry brush, brush egg wash over logs. Cut logs into ⅓″ thick slices and place cookies, 1″ apart, on prepared baking sheet. Bake in oven for 15 to 18 minutes, or until lightly golden.

CHAI BANANA BREAD
Makes 1 loaf

1¾ C. flour
1 T. baking powder
½ tsp. salt
¾ C. sugar
½ C. cream cheese

2 eggs
¾ C. mashed ripe bananas
¼ C. brewed Chai tea

Preheat oven to 350°. In a medium bowl, combine flour, baking powder and salt. In a separate bowl, cream together sugar, cream cheese and eggs, stirring until mixture is lightened and fluffy. Mix in mashed ripe bananas and Chai tea. Add flour mixture and stir until well combined. Pour batter into a greased 5 x 9″ loaf pan. Bake in oven for 60 minutes. Remove from oven and let cool on a wire rack before removing loaf from pan.

GINGER TANGERINE BREAD SQUARES

Makes 12 servings

2 eggs
¼ C. sugar
¼ C. honey
¼ C. molasses
1 C. vegetable oil
½ tsp. cinnamon
½ tsp. ground ginger
½ tsp. salt

½ T. baking soda
10 C. flour, sifted
½ pot tangerine tea,
   brewed strong
3 C. whipped topping
1½ tsp. Chinese Five
   Spice seasoning

Preheat oven to 325°. In a large bowl, combine eggs and sugar. Add honey, molasses and vegetable oil, mixing well. Mix in cinnamon, ground ginger, salt, baking soda and sifted flour. Slowly add strong brewed tea to batter, mixing thoroughly. Pour batter into a greased and floured 9 x 13″ baking dish. Bake in oven for 30 minutes. Meanwhile, in a medium bowl, combine whipped topping and Chinese Five Spice seasoning. Remove gingerbread from oven. Let cool slightly on a wire rack before cutting into squares. Serve each square with a dollop of the whipped topping mixture.

LAPSANG SOUCHONG EGG SALAD SANDWICHES
Makes 4 to 6 servings

3 tsp. Lapsang Souchong tea leaves	2 tsp. finely chopped chives
8 hard-boiled eggs	Pinch of salt, optional
3 T. mayonnaise	8 slices bread, any kind

Prepare Lapsang Souchong tea by placing tea in boiling water for about 10 minutes, letting steep until tea is strong. Peel hard-boiled eggs and place in a large bowl. Pour strong tea over eggs in bowl. Place bowl in refrigerator and let eggs marinate for 36 hours. Remove eggs to a separate bowl and mash coarsely with a spatula. Add mayonnaise and chopped chives, mixing until evenly incorporated. If desired, mix in salt. Spread 2 tablespoons egg mixture over 4 slices of bread. Cover with remaining 4 slices of bread. Cut each sandwich into 4 triangles.

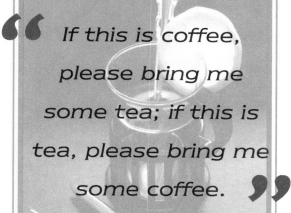

> *If this is coffee, please bring me some tea; if this is tea, please bring me some coffee.*
>
> **Abraham Lincoln**

TEA SMOKED CHICKEN SANDWICHES

Makes 4 to 6 sandwiches

6 T. Lapsang Souchong tea leaves

1 C. soy sauce

¾ C. balsamic vinegar

5 cloves garlic, chopped, divided

1 T. finely chopped fresh gingerroot

½ C. brown sugar

1 orange, halved and juiced

1 lemon, halved and juiced

Salt and pepper to taste

2 lbs. boneless chicken breast

6 oz. goat cheese

1 C. assorted chopped herbs (tarragon, chervil, thyme, chives)

¼ C. whole milk

Chinese Five Spice seasoning

7-grain bread, or any kind

Granny Smith apple slices

Brew tea in about 12 ounces hot water. When tea is finished steeping, add enough ice to make about 14 ounces of tea. In a large bowl, combine tea, soy sauce, balsamic vinegar, 4 cloves chopped garlic, chopped gingerroot, brown sugar, orange juice, lemon juice, salt and pepper. Place chicken in bowl and marinate in refrigerator for at least 4 hours. Preheat oven to 450°. Meanwhile, in a medium mixing bowl, combine goat cheese, remaining chopped garlic and assorted chopped herbs. Stir continuously while adding whole milk, until the mixture is spreadable. Add salt and pepper to taste. To smoke chicken, it is best to use either a perforated pan or a fish poacher. On the bottom of the pan or poacher, spread a small handful of brewed tea leaves. Place the chicken in the pan or poacher and sprinkle both sides with salt, pepper and Chinese Five Spice. Place chicken in oven for 25 to 30 minutes and cook until internal temperature of chicken is 170°. The tea should dry out and smoke the chicken while cooking. Chill smoked chicken in refrigerator. To prepare sandwich, spread a generous amount of goat cheese mixture over bread. Thinly slice the apples and smoked chicken and place on sandwich.

CHARACTERISTICS OF TEA

The following descriptions of some of the world's teas can help you decide your brew of choice. Taste, of course, is a subjective experience, so the best way to discover your favorite is by sampling from the vast world of tea available.

BLACK TEA

Darjeeling
The champagne of teas, with a light body and golden or amber color. Darjeelings can have a sweet grape flavor or a more crisp astringent flavor. Requires precision in steeping.

Lapsang Souchong
One of the world's most famous teas, it is smoked over pine fires. This tea has a smoky, tarry aroma and flavor. Winston Churchill took his with Scotch.

Keemun
The original English breakfast tea. Keemuns are rich with an earthy sweetness and a hint of smokiness.

OOLONG TEA

Formosa oolong
A smooth, medium-bodied tea with a hint of ripe fruit taste.

Wuyi
A floral flavor tea that is light in color with a tint of green.

GREEN TEA

Dragonwell
A yellowish, green tea with a sweet grassy taste.

Gen mai cha
Sometimes called popcorn tea, it is blended with puffed brown rice and has a toasted flavor.

Gyokuro
Called precious dew, this is the finest tea made in Japan. The leaves are deep green and produce a light green tea with a sweet taste.

Matcha
Used in traditional Japanese tea ceremonies, this tea is thick and frothy with a bitter taste.

WHITE TEA

Yin Zhen
Also called silver needles, this tea is the most exotic and expensive tea harvested.

Pai Mu Tan
Made from large leaves, this tea has a smooth, mellow and flowery taste.

PU'ERH TEA

Pu'erh
A dark, black tea with a smooth, rich and earthy flavor.

TEA PARTY POPCORN

Makes 2½ quarts

2½ quarts popped
   popcorn
¼ C. butter, melted

2 T. instant lemon iced
   tea mix
1 T. sugar

In a large bowl, place popped popcorn. Drizzle melted butter over popcorn and toss until evenly coated. In a small bowl, combine instant lemon iced tea mix and sugar. Sprinkle sugar mixture over popcorn and toss again until coated.

GINSENG MUFFINS
Makes 1 dozen

1¼ C. milk
4 tea bags with ginseng
2½ C. flour
⅓ C. sugar

1½ tsp. baking powder
¾ C. cold butter, cut into
    pieces

Preheat oven to 400°. Lightly grease 12 muffin cups and set aside. In a small saucepan over medium low heat, combine milk and tea bags. Heat, stirring occasionally, until bubbles form around the edge of the saucepan. Remove from heat and let mixture cool for about 15 to 20 minutes. Remove tea bags, squeezing any excess liquid back into saucepan, and set mixture aside. In a medium bowl, combine flour, sugar and baking powder. Using a pastry blender, cut in butter pieces until mixture forms coarse crumbs. Add milk mixture, stirring until just moistened. Fill muffin cups ⅔ full with batter mixture and bake in oven for 20 minutes. Remove from oven and let cool slightly before removing from muffin tin.

SPECKLED BREAD

Makes 1 mini loaf

¾ C. raisins or other
   dried fruit
1 C. dark brown sugar
1 C. strong brewed tea

1¼ C. self-rising flour,
   sifted
1 egg, beaten

In a medium bowl, combine dried fruit, brown sugar and brewed tea. Mix well and let mixture soak overnight. Pre-heat oven to 300°. Add sifted flour and beaten egg to fruit mixture. Mix well and pour mixture into a well greased mini loaf tin. Spread batter evenly and bake in oven for 90 min-utes, or until a toothpick inserted in center of loaf comes out clean. Remove from oven, let cool, cover tin and store in refrigerator for 2 days.

SPICED CHAI STUFFING
Makes 8 servings

4 Chai spice tea bags
½ C. boiling water
1 T. olive oil
½ C. chopped celery
½ C. chopped green
  onions

½ C. chopped shallots
1 (7½ oz.) bag
  unseasoned bread cubes
2 eggs
½ tsp. salt
½ tsp. pepper

Preheat oven to 300°. In a glass measuring cup, place Chai spice tea bags. Pour boiling water over tea and let steep for 5 minutes. Remove tea bags, squeezing any excess liquid back into measuring cup. In a medium saucepan over medium heat, combine olive oil, chopped celery, chopped green onions and chopped shallots. Sauté until vegetables are softened. In a large baking dish, combine sautéed vegetables, bread crumbs, eggs, salt, pepper and brewed Chai tea. Mix well and bake in oven for 30 minutes. Serve stuffing as a side dish or use as a stuffing for meat.

GARLIC MASHED POTATOES
Makes 10 to 12 servings

3 lbs. russet potatoes
Salt to taste
6 lemon flavored tea
  bags, divided

1 T. sliced garlic
½ C. butter
2 T. milk

Peel potatoes and cut into cubes. In a large pot over medium high heat, place potatoes. Add salt to taste and enough water to cover potatoes in pot. Add 4 lemon flavored tea bags and sliced garlic to water. Bring to a boil, reduce heat and let simmer until potatoes are softened. Drain potatoes, removing tea bags and garlic slices. Transfer cooked potatoes to a large bowl. Add butter and milk. Carefully cut open tea bags and add loose tea from bags to potatoes. Using a potato masher or hand mixer, mash potatoes until mixture reaches desired consistency.

LEMON SAUTÉED MUSHROOMS

Makes about 2 cups

4 C. fresh sliced
  mushrooms
3 C. water

1 T. fresh sliced garlic
1 T. butter or margarine
2 lemon flavored tea bags

In a large saucepan over medium heat, combine fresh sliced mushrooms, water and minced garlic. Sauté until mushrooms are softened and heated throughout. Drain saucepan, removing water and garlic slices. Return to heat and add butter to sautéed mushrooms. Carefully cut open tea bags and add loose tea from bags to saucepan. Sauté for an additional 5 minutes before serving.

AFTERNOON TEA

*My copper kettle
whistles merrily
and signals that
it is time for tea.*

*The fine china cups
are filled with the brew.
There's lemon and sugar
and sweet cream, too.*

*But, best of all
there's friendship,
between you and me.
as we lovingly share
our afternoon tea.*

Marianna Arolin

HIGH TEA

The term "High Tea" is often misused because people think the name sounds lofty and regal. High Tea, in fact, refers to tea that was served at a high dining table rather than a low tea table. During the Industrial Revolution, the second half of the Victorian Era, working class families would return home exhausted after a long day. The table would be set with foods like Welsh rabbit, shepherd's pie, steak, bread, butter, potatoes, pickles, cheese and tea.

LOW TEA

Also known as Afternoon Tea, Low Tea was usually taken late in the afternoon. It was taken in the sitting room where low tables, like coffee tables, were placed near chairs and sofas. Tiny tea sandwiches, scones and pastries were served with Afternoon Tea. These finger foods were ideal, as the small bites allowed for guests to easily maintain conversation.

TEA ROOMS

As tea became more popular, Tea Rooms sprang up throughout England and many served tea daily from 3 to 5 in the afternoon. Today most Tea Rooms offer three basic types of Afternoon Tea:

Cream Tea – tea served with scones, jam and cream.
Light Tea – tea served with scones and sweets.
Full Tea – tea served with savories, scones and dessert.

GRILLED PORK CHOPS WITH TANGY TEA SAUCE

Makes 4 servings

1 C. prepared mustard
½ C. brown sugar
¼ C. unsweetened
  instant tea powder
2 T. water
2 T. honey

2 tsp. hot pepper sauce
1 tsp. liquid smoke,
  optional
4 (½˝ thick) pork loin
  chops

Preheat grill to high heat and lightly oil the grate. In a small saucepan over medium heat, combine mustard, brown sugar, instant tea powder, water, honey, hot pepper sauce and, if desired, liquid smoke. Heat, stirring with a wire whisk, until mixture begins to boil. Grill pork loin chops, turning once, until no longer pink in the middle. To serve, place pork chops on a serving platter and drizzle tea sauce over top. Serve immediately.

PAPAYA BEEF SKEWERS
Makes 4 servings

¼ C. sweet chili sauce
3 T. Maggi seasoning
sauce
2 T. loose green tea
leaves or green tea
powder
1 T. rice vinegar
1 T. sugar
1 T. papaya seeds

1 lb. beef tenderloin,
cut into 1˝ cubes
½ large papaya, peeled
and seeded, cut into
1˝ cubes
1 medium white onion,
cut into 1˝ cubes
8 (10˝) skewers

In a medium bowl, combine sweet chili sauce, seasoning sauce, green tea leaves, rice vinegar, sugar and papaya seeds. Mix well and add cubed beef. Toss until evenly coated, cover and chill in refrigerator for 2 hours or overnight. Preheat grill to medium heat and lightly oil the grate. Slide marinated beef, cubed papaya and cubed onions onto skewers. Place kabobs on grill and heat for 4 to 7 minutes, or until beef is no longer pink and onions are tender.

BLACK BEAN SOUP

Makes 4 servings

1 onion, chopped
1 T. vegetable oil
2 cloves garlic, minced
1 C. water
1 (15 oz.) can black beans
1 (14 oz.) can diced
  tomatoes in juice

$^1/_3$ C. white rice
Salt and pepper to taste
2 C. strong brewed
  Lapsang Souchong tea

In a large pot over medium high heat, place vegetable oil. Add chopped onion and sauté until onions are softened and slightly brown. Add garlic and sauté for an additional minute. Add water, beans in liquid, tomatoes in juice and rice to pot. Bring mixture to a boil, reduce heat and cover. Let simmer for about 30 minutes, until rice is softened. Add salt and pepper to taste and stir in strong Lapsang Souchong tea. Transfer soup in batches to a blender. Process on high until pureed. Repeat with remaining soup. Serve immediately.

LEMON BLOSSOM CHICKEN LINGUINE
Makes 4 servings

2 T. olive oil
4 boneless, skinless chicken breasts, cut into strips
1 (16 oz.) pkg. frozen mixed vegetables
8 oz. linguine, cooked and drained
1 (8 oz.) pkg. cream cheese
½ C. milk
3 lemon flavored tea bags

In a large skillet over medium heat, place olive oil. Add chicken breast strips and frozen vegetables and sauté for about 15 minutes, or until chicken is cooked throughout. Meanwhile, in a medium saucepan over low heat, combine cream cheese, milk and contents of the lemon tea bags. Let mixture simmer, stirring constantly, until smooth. To serve, place cooked linguine on serving plates. Top each serving with an even amount of the sautéed chicken and vegetables and pour lemon sauce over each.

MINT BRAISED ASPARAGUS TIPS

Makes 4 servings

1 large bundle fresh
  asparagus
1 T. white vinegar
4 medium eggs

½ C. butter
1 mint flavored tea bag
Salt and pepper to taste

Cut stems from asparagus and discard. In a large pot of lightly salted water, place asparagus tips. Cook until asparagus is tender, remove from heat and drain pot. In a separate pot of boiling water, add white vinegar. Poach eggs in boiling water and set aside. In a medium saucepan over medium heat, place butter. Add cooked asparagus tips and sprinkle contents of the mint flavored tea bag over asparagus. When the tea has been absorbed by the butter, remove asparagus to a serving plate and top with poached eggs. Pour melted butter from saucepan over eggs and season with salt and pepper to taste.

MANDARIN ORANGE MEATBALLS

Makes 10 servings

5 mandarin orange spice
  tea bags
1½ C. white wine
1 lb. ground beef
1 lb. ground pork
¼ red onion, diced

4 cloves garlic, minced
Salt and pepper to taste
2 T. olive or corn oil
1 T. cornstarch
1 C. orange marmalade

In a medium bowl, place tea bags. Add white wine and let mixture steep for about 10 minutes. Remove tea bags, squeezing any excess liquid back into bowl. Set wine mixture aside. In a large bowl, combine ground beef, ground pork, diced onion, minced garlic, salt and pepper to taste. Add ¾ cup of the wine mixture and mix until incorporated. Form mixture into about 35 small meatballs. In a large skillet over medium heat, place olive oil. Add meatballs to skillet in batches until browned. Remove meatballs to a plate and keep warm. Drain grease from skillet and add remaining wine mixture, cornstarch and orange marmalade to skillet. Return to medium heat and cook, stirring occasionally, until thickened. Add meatballs to sauce mixture and simmer for about 15 minutes.

TEA ROASTED CHICKEN
Makes 4 servings

2 tsp. kosher salt
1 T. crushed peppercorns
1 (2 to 3 lb.) whole chicken
½ C. loose green tea leaves
½ C. sugar

½ C. uncooked white rice
2 T. soy sauce
2 T. rice vinegar
1 T. chopped shallots
1 T. peanut or vegetable oil
Pinch of sugar

In a medium bowl, combine kosher salt and crushed peppercorns. Rub mixture over entire chicken, cover and marinate in refrigerator for 1 hour. Remove chicken from refrigerator and let stand at room temperature for 30 minutes. Meanwhile, line a large Dutch oven with 2 layers of aluminum foil. Spread green tea leaves, sugar and rice over aluminum foil. Place a small wire rack over ingredients on foil and place 4 wooden chopsticks in a crisscross pattern over wire rack, breaking sticks to fit Dutch oven if necessary. Place whole chicken over chopsticks and cover top of Dutch oven with another layer of aluminum foil and a heavy lid. Cook chicken over high heat for 10 to 14 minutes, until smoke begins to form inside Dutch oven. Reduce heat to medium and cook for an additional 10 minutes. Remove from heat and let stand, covered, for 10 minutes. Uncover chicken and carefully transfer to a large roasting pan, discarding rice mixture in bottom of Dutch oven. In a medium bowl, whisk together soy sauce, rice vinegar, chopped shallots, peanut oil and a pinch of sugar. Mix well and brush mixture over chicken. Roast in oven for 15 minutes, brushing occasionally with additional soy sauce mixture. Continue to roast for an additional 15 minutes, or until chicken thigh registers 180° on a meat thermometer. Remove from oven and let stand for 5 minutes before slicing chicken.

USING EDIBLE FLOWERS IN TEA

Using edible flowers in various foods and drinks can be a beautiful and appetizing way to enhance the taste and appearance of the dish. Some common plants with edible flowers are: dandelion, lilac, nasturtium, tulip, violet, pansy, yucca, signet marigold, African marigold, garden sage, rose, rosemary, garden pea, scented geranium, grape hyacinth, mint, apple, crabapple, lavender, daylily, chrysanthemum, squash, pumpkin, orange, oxeye daisy, lemon, safflower, broccoli, English daisy, chive and hollyhock.

An idea for using edible flowers in tea is to freeze the flowers or mint leaves with water in ice cube trays. Add the frozen cubes to a pitcher of iced tea just before serving. Freezing the flowers with water in a ring mold and adding to a punch bowl would also make a beautiful presentation.

Try wrapping thin strips of orange or lemon peel around skewers of berries and adding the sticks to hot or cold tea. Float fruit slices or edible flowers on top of a single cup of hot or cold tea. Edible flowers also make a nice garnish for foods served with tea, such as sprinkled over a tea cake or on a plate of tea sandwiches or cookies.

Be sure to use edible flowers that are free of both natural and manmade toxins. If using flowers from a garden, make sure that no chemical fertilizers or pesticides were used on the plants or nearby soil. Use the flowers immediately after they have been picked. Remove the stems and leaves and rinse the blooms under cool water. Gently pat dry the petals. In some cases, edible flowers are available in the produce section of supermarkets.

APRICOT GLAZED CHICKEN WINGS

Makes 12 wings

⅔ C. apricot preserves
1 T. unsweetened instant
  tea powder

12 chicken wings

Preheat broiler. Line a baking sheet with aluminum foil and place chicken wings in an even layer on baking sheet. In a blender, combine apricot preserves and instant tea powder. Pulse until smooth and, using a pastry brush, brush mixture generously over chicken wings on baking sheet. Place under broiler and brush occasionally with additional glaze sauce. Broil for 12 to 15 minutes on each side, or until no longer pink in the middle.

SEAFOOD CHOWDER
Makes 4 servings

1 T. olive oil
3 C. peeled and cubed
potatoes
1 (12 oz.) can mushrooms,
drained
1 (12 oz.) bag scallops or
other seafood
1 tsp. chicken bouillon
granules

½ tsp. salt
½ tsp. pepper
4 lemon flavored tea bags,
divided
1 (8 oz.) pkg. cream cheese
½ C. evaporated milk
1 T. butter
2 C. water

In a large soup pot over medium heat, place olive oil. Add potatoes, mushrooms, scallops, chicken bouillon, salt and pepper. Cut open 1 tea bag and add contents to pot. Heat for about 20 minutes, stirring occasionally, until all ingredients are cooked throughout. Meanwhile, in a small saucepan over low heat, combine cream cheese, evaporated milk, butter and contents of the remaining 3 tea bags. Simmer for about 15 minutes, stirring occasionally with a wire whisk, until creamy and smooth. Add cream cheese mixture and water to soup pot. Mix well, reduce heat and simmer for an additional 20 minutes.

TEA-SMOKED STEAK
Makes 1 serving

2 T. basmati rice
4 tea bags

4 T. brown sugar
1 sirloin steak

Line a wok with aluminum foil and place basmati rice and brown sugar on foil. Carefully cut open tea bags and place contents from bags on foil. Place a rack in wok so it rests about 2″ to 3″ over aluminum foil layer. Heat wok until ingredients begin to smoke and place sirloin steak on rack inside wok. Cover with a lid and let steak smoke for 10 to 15 minutes, or until steak reaches desired doneness.

Tea does our fancy aid,

Repress those vapours

which the head invade

And keeps that palace

of the soul serene.

Edmund Waller

SLOW COOKER ROAST WITH MANGO SAUCE

Makes 10 to 12 servings

4 mango passionfruit tea bags	1 C. corn syrup
½ C. boiling water	1/3 C. brown sugar
	1 large beef rump roast

In a tea pot or bowl, place mango passionfruit tea bags. Pour boiling water over tea bags and let steep for 4 minutes. Remove tea bags, squeezing any excess liquid back into the tea pot. In a medium saucepan over medium high heat, place brewed tea, corn syrup and brown sugar. Mix well and simmer for 1 minute. Bring mixture to a boil and remove from heat. Place rump roast in crock pot and pour sauce over roast. Cook at low setting for 8 to 10 hours.

HERBED HALIBUT
Makes 4 servings

1 lb. halibut or other
  white fish
4 T. milk
4 T. white wine
Salt and pepper to taste

Garlic powder to taste
2 lemon flavored tea bags,
  divided
¼ C. sliced mushrooms
¼ C. sliced onions

Preheat oven to 325°. Lightly grease a 9 x 13″ baking dish and place halibut in dish. Add milk and white wine and sprinkle with salt, pepper and garlic powder to taste. Carefully open 1 lemon flavored tea bag and sprinkle contents of bag over fish. Place sliced onions and sliced mushrooms over fish and sprinkle again with salt, pepper and garlic powder to taste. Sprinkle the contents of the remaining tea bag over mushrooms and onions. Place lid over baking dish and bake in oven for 25 minutes, checking fish after 20 minutes. Fish is done when it flakes easily with a fork.

CURRIED CHICKPEAS

Makes 6 servings

2 C. water
1 tea bag
1 bay leaf
2 (15 oz.) cans garbanzo
   beans, drained
2 T. vegetable oil, divided
2 onions, 1 sliced and
   1 minced, divided
3 tomatoes, chopped,
   divided
¼ C. fresh chopped
   cilantro

1 tsp. ground coriander
1 tsp. cumin seed
1 tsp. fresh grated
   gingerroot
1 tsp. minced garlic
1 tsp. ground turmeric,
   optional
Salt and cayenne pepper
   to taste

In a medium pot over medium high heat, place water, tea bag and bay leaf. Bring mixture to a boil. Set aside ½ cup of the garbanzo beans and add remaining garbanzo beans to pot. When beans are cooked throughout, remove tea bag and bay leaf. Remove pot from heat and drain beans, reserving the water. In a medium skillet over medium heat, place 2 teaspoons vegetable oil. Add sliced onion and sauté until onion is tender. Remove from heat and let cool. Stir reserved ½ cup garbanzo beans into onions. Add 1 chopped tomato and half of the chopped cilantro. Mix well and set aside. In a large skillet over medium high heat, place remaining vegetable oil. Add ground coriander, cumin seeds, gingerroot and garlic. Sauté for about 15 to 20 seconds, or until lightly browned. If desired, stir in turmeric. Add minced onion and sauté until tender. Mix in remaining chopped tomatoes and season with salt and cayenne pepper to taste. Bring to a boil and cook for about 5 minutes. Add cooked garbanzo beans, sliced onion mixture and enough of the reserved cooking water until mixture is thick and has a consistency of gravy. Heat for an additional 5 minutes, stirring occasionally. Garnish with remaining chopped cilantro and serve immediately.

RASPBERRY GLAZED
PORK LOIN
Makes 2 servings

1 C. corn syrup
⅓ C. brown sugar
4 raspberry flavored
  tea bags

½ C. boiling water
1 medium pork loin, scored

Preheat oven to 350°. In a medium saucepan over medium heat, combine corn syrup and brown sugar. Mix well and simmer for 1 minute. In a teapot or bowl, place raspberry flavored tea bags. Pour boiling water over tea bags and let steep for 4 minutes. Remove tea bags, squeezing any excess liquid back into tea pot. Add tea to saucepan and bring to a boil, stirring occasionally. Remove from heat and let cool. Place scored pork loin in a medium baking dish and pour glaze mixture over loin. Bake in oven for 2½ hours, or until syrup is evaporated and loin is glazed and cooked throughout.

DILL SALMON DIP
Makes

1¾ C. smoked salmon,
   skinned and boned
⅔ C. butter, softened
2 lemon flavored tea bags

1 T. water
2 tsp. fresh chopped
   dillweed
Salt and pepper to taste

Into a medium bowl, flake the smoked salmon with a fork. Add butter, contents of lemon flavored tea bags, water and fresh chopped dill. Continue to mix with a fork and season with salt and pepper to taste. Transfer mixture to a blender or food processor. Process on high until mixture is very smooth. Pour mixture into a small serving bowl. Serve salmon dip with various crackers, bread sticks or raw vegetables for dipping.

APPLE CINNAMON TEA BARS
Makes 12 servings

1 C. plus 2 T. flour, divided
1¼ C. powdered sugar, divided
½ C. plus 3 T. butter, melted, divided
1 C. sugar
1 C. shredded coconut

1 (8 oz.) pkg. cream cheese, softened
2 eggs
½ tsp. baking powder
¼ tsp. salt
12 apple cinnamon tea bags, divided
1 T. water

Preheat oven to 375°. In a medium bowl, combine 1 cup flour, ¼ cup powdered sugar and ½ cup butter, mixing until coarse crumbs form. Press mixture into bottom of a greased 9 x 13″ baking dish. Bake in oven for 7 to 10 minutes. In a medium bowl, combine sugar, shredded coconut, cream cheese, eggs, baking powder, salt, contents of 10 tea bags and remaining 2 tablespoons flour. Mix in 2 tablespoons butter, stirring until blended. Spread over crust and return to oven for 15 to 20 minutes, or until filling is set. In a medium bowl, combine 1 cup powdered sugar, 1 tablespoon melted butter, contents of remaining 2 tea bags and water. Mix and spread over filling while warm.

PEACH TEA COBBLER
Makes 12 to 16 servings

4 C. peach flavored water	8 T. cornstarch
10 peach flavored tea bags	4 C. Bisquick baking mix
8 C. fresh or frozen sliced peaches	2 C. milk
1 C. plus 6 T. brown sugar	2 eggs
	Whipped topping

Preheat oven to 350°. In a large saucepan over medium high heat, bring peach water to a boil. Add tea bags and continue to boil for 5 minutes. Remove from heat and discard tea bags, squeezing any excess liquid back into saucepan. Over the bottom of a 9 x 13″ baking dish, spread sliced peaches in an even layer. Sprinkle 1 cup brown sugar and cornstarch over peaches and pour tea mixture over all. In a medium mixing bowl, combine baking mix, remaining 6 tablespoons brown sugar, milk and eggs. Stir until a dough is formed. Drop table-spoonfuls of the dough mixture over peaches. Bake in oven for 45 minutes, or until topping is golden brown. Remove from oven and serve immediately. Top each serving with a dollop of whipped topping.

*" Thank God for tea!
What would the world
do without tea! How did
it exist? I am glad I was
not born before tea. "*

William Gladstone

BLACKCURRANT ICE CREAM CAKE

Makes 1 (9″) cake

¾ C. superfine sugar
¾ C. butter, softened
3 eggs
1½ C. self-rising flour
2½ pints vanilla ice cream, softened

2½ C. heavy whipping cream
4 blackcurrant tea bags, divided
2 C. fresh currants

Preheat oven to 350°. In a medium bowl, combine sugar, butter and flour. Stir until mixture is lightened and fluffy. Carefully cut open 2 tea bags and add loose tea from bags to mixture. Mix in eggs, stirring until well combined. Pour mixture into a greased 9″ square baking dish, spreading evenly. Bake in oven for 20 to 25 minutes. Remove from oven and turn out onto a wire rack to cool. Cut cake horizontally to make two thin layers. Place one cake layer on a serving platter and spread softened ice cream over cake. Top with remaining cake layer and place in freezer for 3 to 4 hours. Meanwhile, in a medium mixing bowl, beat heavy whipping cream and contents of remaining 2 tea bags until stiff peaks form. Quickly spread whipped cream over top and sides of cake and return to freezer. To serve, remove cake from freezer and let sit for 10 minutes. Garnish with fresh currants.

LAYERED GREEN TEA CAKE

Makes 1 (9″) cake

1 C. flour
1 C. cake flour
1 tsp. baking soda
1 tsp. salt
6 tsp. green tea powder,
    divided
1¼ C. sugar
1 C. vegetable oil

3 eggs
1 C. plain yogurt
2 tsp. vanilla, divided
1¼ C. powdered sugar
2 T. butter, softened
1 (3 oz.) pkg. cream
    cheese, softened
1½ tsp. milk

Preheat oven to 350°. Grease and lightly flour two 9″ round cake pans. Into a medium bowl, sift flour, cake flour, baking soda, salt and 4 teaspoons green tea powder. In a large bowl, whisk together sugar, vegetable oil and eggs, mixing until smooth. Stir in 1½ teaspoons vanilla. Alternating, add yogurt and dry mixture, beating well after each addition. Pour batter evenly into prepared pans. Bake in oven for 30 to 40 minutes, or until a toothpick inserted in center of cakes comes out clean. Meanwhile, to prepare frosting, in a medium mixing bowl, combine powdered sugar and remaining 2 teaspoons green tea powder. Add butter, cream cheese, milk and remaining ½ teaspoon vanilla and beat at high speed until smooth. Remove cake from oven and let cool completely. To assemble, place one cake layer on a serving platter. Spread a thin layer of frosting over cake and top with remaining cake layer. Spread remaining frosting over top and sides of cake.

MANGO TEA ICE CREAM
Makes 5 cups

⅔ C. cold water
4 mango flavored tea bags
4 very firm green mangoes

⅔ C. sugar
2 C. heavy whipping cream
3 T. dry milk powder

In a large saucepan over medium high heat, bring water to a rapid boil. Add tea bags and let steep for 5 minutes. Remove from heat and discard tea bags. Peel mangoes and remove seeds. Dice mango flesh into small pieces and add to tea in saucepan. Sprinkle sugar over diced mango and return to medium high heat. Cook, stirring often, until fruit is very soft. Using a fork, mash mangoes to form a course puree. Remove from heat and drain any excess liquid from saucepan. Set aside to cool. Meanwhile, in a medium mixing bowl, beat heavy cream and dry milk powder until stiff peaks form. Gently fold mango puree into whipped cream and transfer mixture to a plastic freezer container. Cover and place in freezer until ice cream is solid.

CHAMOMILE SANGRIA
Makes 6 servings

6 C. cold water
14 chamomile herb tea bags
1 C. halved green seedless grapes
1 C. orange sections
1 C. quartered strawberries

1 C. pineapple chunks
1½ C. pineapple juice, chilled
1½ C. cranberry juice, chilled
1 C. orange juice, chilled
2 C. ginger ale, chilled
Shaved ice

In a large saucepan over medium high heat, bring water to a rapid boil. Add tea bags and let steep for 10 minutes. Remove from heat and discard tea bags. Let tea cool to room temperature. In a large pitcher, place halved grapes, orange sections, quartered strawberries and pineapple chunks. Pour pineapple juice, cranberry juice, ginger ale and tea over fruit in pitcher. Chill in refrigerator at least 4 hours before serving. To serve, pour sangria into tall glasses filled with shaved ice.

> **"** *My dear, if you could give me a cup of tea to clear my muddle of a head I should better understand your affairs.* **"**
>
> **Charles Dickens**

APPLE CINNAMON CHEESECAKE
Makes 1 (9˝) cheesecake

6 apple cinnamon tea
  bags
2 (8 oz.) pkgs. cream
  cheese, softened

½ C. sugar
2 eggs
1 (9˝) prepared graham
  cracker pie crust

Preheat oven to 350°. In a large mixing bowl, combine contents of apple cinnamon tea bags, cream cheese and sugar. Beat at high speed and add eggs, mixing until well blended. Pour mixture into prepared pie crust. Bake in oven for 40 minutes. Remove from oven and chill in refrigerator at least 3 hours before serving.

CHAI TEA MERINGUES
Makes 12 servings

3 egg whites
1 C. sugar
½ tsp. ground
  cardamom

¼ tsp. cinnamon
¼ tsp. ground cloves
1 tsp. instant tea powder

Preheat oven to 250°. In a large mixing bowl, beat egg whites at low speed until foamy. Increase to high speed and beat until stiff peaks form. Gradually add sugar and continue beating at high speed. Carefully fold in ground cardamom, cinnamon, ground cloves and instant tea powder, mixing as little as possible. Drop mixture in small mounds onto parchment or aluminum foil lined baking sheets. Bake in oven for 90 minutes. Turn off oven heat and let meringues sit in oven overnight or until oven has completely cooled, being careful not to open oven door. Remove from baking sheets and store in an airtight container.

LEMON TEA BISCOTTI
Makes about 12 servings

3¾ C. flour
1 tsp. baking powder
½ tsp. salt
1 C. sugar
1 C. butter or margarine,
    softened
4 eggs

1 tsp. vanilla
1½ tsp. grated lemon
    peel
¼ C. unsweetened
    instant tea powder
2 T. water
¾ C. chopped pecans

Preheat oven to 350°. Lightly grease two baking sheets and set aside. In a medium bowl, combine flour, baking powder and salt. In a large bowl, combine sugar and butter at medium speed. Add eggs, one at a time, beating well. Stir in lemon peel and vanilla. In a small bowl, combine tea powder and water, mixing until tea is dissolved. Add tea mixture to sugar mixture and gradually mix in flour mixture and chopped pecans. Shape dough into two 2 x 11″ logs and place each on baking sheets. Bake for 20 minutes, or until a toothpick inserted in center of biscotti comes out clean. Remove from oven and cut into ½″ thick slices. Place slices, cut side down, on baking sheets and bake for 20 to 25 minutes, turning once during baking time. Remove from oven and let cool.

CINNAMON APPLE TEA CRISP
Makes 6 servings

2 cinnamon apple flavored
  tea bags
1/3 C. cold water
5 C. peeled and sliced
  apples
3/4 C. flour

1 C. sugar
1/4 tsp. cinnamon
1/4 tsp. salt, optional
1/2 C. butter, cut into
  pieces
Vanilla ice cream, optional

Preheat oven to 350°. In a medium saucepan over medium high heat, bring water to a boil. Add tea bags and let steep for 3 minutes. Remove from heat, discarding tea bags, and let tea cool. Grease a 9″ square baking dish and arrange apple slices evenly in bottom of dish. Pour tea over apples. In a medium bowl, combine flour, sugar, cinnamon and, if desired, salt. Using a pastry blender, cut in butter until mixture is crumbly. Sprinkle mixture evenly over apples in baking dish. Bake in oven for 30 minutes, or until topping is lightly browned. To serve, cut apple crisp into squares and, if desired, serve each with a scoop of vanilla ice cream.

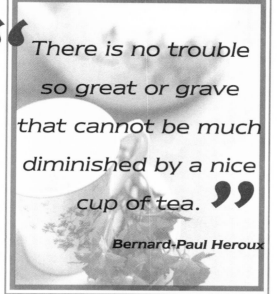

There is no trouble so great or grave that cannot be much diminished by a nice cup of tea.

Bernard-Paul Heroux

HAZELNUT CHOCOLATE TEA CAKE
Makes 1 (9″) bundt cake

4 eggs, separated
1 C. butter, softened
1⅔ C. sugar
1 C. brewed black tea, chilled

2 C. flour
1½ T. baking powder
⅓ C. dry breadcrumbs
⅓ C. cocoa powder
1 C. chopped hazelnuts

Preheat oven to 360°. Grease and flour a 9″ bundt cake pan and set aside. In a large bowl, cream together egg yolks, butter and sugar, mixing until lightened and fluffy. Gradually mix in cold black tea. In a separate bowl, combine flour, baking powder, bread crumbs, cocoa powder and chopped hazelnuts. Toss until well combined and fold mixture into butter mixture, stirring until just mixed. In a large mixing bowl, beat egg whites at high speed until stiff peaks form. Fold egg whites into batter mixture and pour batter into prepared pan. Bake in oven for 60 to 70 minutes, or until a toothpick inserted in center of cake comes out clean. Remove from oven and let cake cool for 20 minutes before turning out on a wire rack.

LEMON TEA BARS
Makes 12 servings

1 C. plus 2 T. flour, divided
1¼ C. powdered sugar, divided
½ C. plus 1 T. butter, softened, divided
1 C. sugar
1 C. shredded coconut

1 (8 oz.) pkg. cream cheese
2 eggs
½ tsp. baking powder
¼ tsp. salt
12 lemon flavored tea bags
1 T. lemon juice

Preheat oven to 375°. In medium bowl, combine 1 cup flour, ¼ cup powdered sugar and ½ cup butter. Mix well until mixture forms coarse crumbs. Grease a 9 x 13″ baking dish and press mixture into bottom of baking dish. Bake for 7 to 10 minutes, or until lightly browned. To prepare filling, in a medium mixing bowl, combine sugar, shredded coconut and cream cheese. Beat at medium speed until well combined and add eggs, remaining 2 tablespoons flour, baking powder, salt and contents of 10 lemon tea bags. Mix well and spread over crust layer. Return to oven for 15 to 20 minutes. To prepare frosting, in a medium bowl, combine remaining 1 cup powdered sugar, remaining 1 tablespoon butter, contents of remaining 2 tea bags and lemon juice. Mix and spread over filling while still warm.

GREEN TEA PETITS FOURS

Makes 12 servings

1/3 C. cake flour
2 T. cornstarch
1 T. plus 3 tsp. powdered
   green tea, divided
2 eggs
3 egg yolks
8 T. sugar, divided

1/8 tsp. cream of tartar
2 egg whites
Powdered sugar
1 C. heavy whipping cream
4 tsp. superfine sugar
6 T. almond paste

Preheat oven to 450°. Grease a 7 x 11″ baking dish and line with parchment paper. Lightly grease and flour the parchment paper and set aside. Into a medium bowl, sift cake flour, cornstarch and 1 tablespoon powdered green tea. In a large mixing bowl, combine 2 whole eggs, 3 egg yolks and 6 tablespoons sugar. Beat at high speed for about 5 minutes, until mixture has tripled in volume. Fold flour mixture and cream of tartar into beaten egg mixture, mixing until foamy. Add remaining 2 tablespoons sugar and continue beating at high speed until stiff peaks form. Fold 1/3 of the egg whites into the batter, mix well and add remaining egg whites. Spread batter evenly into prepared baking dish. Bake in oven for 8 to 10 minutes, or until a toothpick inserted in center of cake comes out clean. Remove from oven and sprinkle lightly with powdered sugar. Invert cake onto a flat surface and let cool. To make whipped cream, in a medium bowl, beat heavy cream, superfine sugar and 2 teaspoons powdered green tea with a wire whisk. To prepare marzipan, knead together almond paste and remaining 1 teaspoon powdered green tea. Roll out marzipan between two sheets of plastic wrap and lightly dust with powdered sugar while rolling. When cake has cooled, remove parchment paper from cake and cut horizontally to make two thin cake layers. Spread half of the whipped cream over one cake layer and top with remaining cake layer. Spread remaining whipped cream over cake. Cut cake into 12 even squares. Cut marzipan into 12 squares and drape over cake pieces, smoothing down to make a flat, frosted surface.

COCONUT TEA COOKIES
Makes about 5 dozen

1 C. boiling water
4 English breakfast tea
  bags
3 C. flour
1 tsp. baking powder
1 tsp. baking soda
1 tsp. salt

1½ C. butter, softened
1 C. brown sugar
⅔ C. sugar
2 large eggs
1 tsp. vanilla
2 C. shredded coconut,
  divided

Preheat oven to 350°. In a teapot or bowl, combine boiling water and tea bags. Cover and let tea steep for 5 minutes. Remove tea bags and let tea cool to room temperature. In a medium bowl, combine flour, baking powder, baking soda and salt. In a large bowl, combine butter, brown sugar and sugar, beating at high speed until fluffy. Add eggs, vanilla and brewed tea, mixing until just blended. Add flour mixture and continue beating at low speed. Set aside ¼ cup shredded coconut and fold remaining coconut into batter. Drop dough by tablespoonfuls onto greased baking sheets. Sprinkle reserved coconut over cookies and bake for 12 minutes, or until golden brown. Remove from oven and let cool.

INDEX